Buddha
in a
Red Dress

A Refreshing Guide to
Mindfulness, Meditation
and Transformational
Adventures

Melanie Dilday

Disclaimer: The information contained within this publication is strictly for educational purposes. If you wish to apply ideas contained in this book, you are taking full responsibility for your actions. This book is not intended to be a substitute for the medical advice of a licensed physician. The reader should consult with their doctor in any matters relating to his/ her health. The author has made every effort to ensure the accuracy of the information within this book was correct at time of publication. The author does not assume and hereby disclaims any liability to any party for any loss, damage, or disruption caused by errors or omissions, whether such errors or omissions result from accident, negligence, or any other cause. This book is designed to provide information and motivation to our

"This being human is a guest house.
Every morning, a new arrival. A joy,
a depression, a meanness, some
momentary awareness comes as an
unexpected visitor.
Welcome and entertain them all!
Even if they're a crowd of sorrows,
who violently sweep your house
empty of its furniture, still, treat
each guest honorably.
He may be cleaning you out for some
new delight.
The dark thought, the shame, the
malice: meet them at the door
laughing, and invite them in.
Be grateful for whoever comes."
~Rumi

TABLE OF CONTENTS

Acknowledgements

I want to thank all those who came along with me on this amazing journey, however long or short.

To those who caused upset and contraction, you bastards <joking>, I thank you, for giving me an opportunity to grow and to see through the veil of illusion.

To those who brought me light, love, laughter and insight, I thank you, for enabling the best of me to shine.

Special deep hearted gratitude to Meike Schütt, my spiritual 'inviter' on this incredible journey of Truth and exploration of the moment.

Finally, a huge thank you to my dear friends who have loved me through all the highs and lows. Those very same people who continue to support me by encouraging me to write this book and have been instrumental in its successful launching.

Introduction

People are struggling more than ever in today's world to find peace and fulfillment. The fast pace, the poor economy and the relentlessly negative mainstream media lead to ever-growing feelings of isolation in the midst of a crowd.

At times it may seem as if the world is coming apart at the seams and bringing many of us along with it. And yet, there are people who remain unaffected by these challenges.

They aren't special—nor are they always rich or lucky or even particularly intelligent. They're just average people who have decided that there must be more to life than this.

They respond rather than react. They keep still at the centre.

This book delves into the life of one such woman, offering up many of the processes, techniques and insights she's used in order to help those who are ready for change.

As you read through these pages, ask yourself the following questions.

Are you tired of feeling anxious, unloved, helpless, depressed, tethered or disenchanted?

Have you had the realization that there must be more to life but you don't know how or where to start?

Are you already on the path of discovering peace through meditation, personal development or spiritual growth and are hungry to discover more?

This book will do its best to provide answers to these questions and more.

Melanie draws from 30 years experience and exploration in personal growth work, spiritual growth, meditation, mindfulness, therapies and workshops.

People from all walks of life who have implemented some of these processes have found a level of freedom, fulfilment and peace that they could not have previously imagined.

Relationships improve, stress dissolves, life flows and becomes an adventure again.

Penny, small business owner and mother of two children says, "the best thing about this book is that you can read it on a Sunday and by the next Sunday you are already seeing results."

If you choose to delve deeply into just one of a dozen different topics in this book, your life will improve.

As you start to feel better, and more aware, relaxed, and empowered, you will want to unpack and explore some of the other topics because you will be able to taste the freedom.

Don't be satisfied with a lackluster life. Don't put up with feeling needlessly anxious or unfulfilled.

Be the one who takes the next step into freedom beyond your expectations.

All you have to do to improve your life is to keep reading. Each chapter will give you new insight as you explore a new way of living in this world.

Prologue

I was born blue. Literally. My mum was in labour for two days. Finally, I popped out . . . blue. The cord around my neck nearly killed me.

My first two weeks on the planet were spent alone, in a glass cage. In solitary confinement.

A totally fucked up way to start a life.

It wasn't until I turned 56 that I finally got over that. In the safety of a circle of women, the little one inside me finally got to be seen and held.

I couldn't speak. I was pre-speech. I was a newborn. I was a hands-fisting, feet-curling, sobbing newborn at 56 years of age.

That process in the women's circle was the final piece of the puzzle for me. It was only then that my life began anew.

Suddenly I was free of need and loneliness. I was free of all the things that had underpinned my motivations. I was free of the undercurrent of neediness that weaved through oh so many of my previous relationships.

I was even free of the need to depend upon a relationship for my happiness.

All of which has brought me here to Ubud in Bali, Indonesia, the perfect place to start writing a book. Unlike the woman in "Eat, Pray, Love", I did not come to Ubud in search of answers.

I have come to that point in life where I no longer have the need to search for answers. I am no longer searching for Love, searching for God, searching for food, drugs, wealth, praise, or peace. I am complete, right here, right now.

And this is the story of how I got here.

The reason I decided to write this book is because if I can get here, so can you. I want to share my journey, the techniques and processes I learned (and continue to learn) that enables me to be happy, wild and free . . . so that you can be free too.

I'm just like you. There is nothing at all special about me. I come from a middle class upbringing. I've been married and divorced, twice.

I studied Psychology for a short time, did some personal growth courses, taught meditation in a little room in Mandurah, Australia for a time, got into art and taught that too.

I've had all kinds of jobs—from barmaid to finance manager, dental nurse to leasing executive. I haven't made a fortune, but was able to live comfortably enough.

I lived a work-hard, pay-the-bills type of life . . . . by all accounts I'm pretty 'normal' right? Only thing is I always felt like something was missing. I was doing okay and was pretty happy, but I knew there were 'cracks' in my life and I wasn't totally at peace.

I knew that there must be more to life than driving bumper-to-bumper on the freeway from work every day only to come home to an empty house or an empty relationship.

Well, I'm here to tell you that it doesn't have to be like that. If I was able to go from empty to full, from restlessness to peace, from unconsciousness to awareness, from lackluster to bright shining light . . . then so can you.

A Special Gift

FREE 20 minute Guided Meditation

REST IN THIS THAT YOU ARE:
A Guided Meditation in Resting as
Awareness

From the audio: "You are much more than the body, much more than the mind. You are awareness itself. All there really is, is a sense of presence. When a thought arises, it is only a movement. No need to follow it. You are simply the space in which all movements happen. Like the sky. Clouds come and go like thoughts, but the sky is always present.

You are just here like the ever present sky..."

Download from here:
http://livelifehappy.today/meditations/

Chapter One:
Ask and It Will Be Given

I wake up to the sounds of scratching noises. Monkey Dog wags his tail as I open the door. He nudges my thighs and leans into me. My heart opens, liquid with love.

He's like no other dog I have ever encountered. He's the epitome of freedom and it is so fitting that he came into my life at a time when I too am truly free.

Monkey Dog has six people who love and care for him. He has several names. Rouge, Ketut, Habib, Ollie, Hans . . . and now Monkey Dog. He's a very multicultural dog! He roams freely, spreading the love.

My Palestinian neighbour tells the story of how he adopted him and named him Habib. He was at a yoga class one morning with his dog and called out "Habib" when a French guy next to him said, "that's not his name, he's called Rouge." "No, no, it's Habib."

They quickly realised that this dog was living at both places. Over time, it was discovered that there were three other 'owners' (one the 'actual' owner).

Roaming freely from place to place, Monkey Dog comes and goes, sometimes he just wants a pat or something to eat. Other times hanging out for days.

He looks very much like an Australian Dingo with a bit of White Labrador thrown in. Even his nature has the freedom of the dingo and the gentleness of a lab.

He's so special that all the owners get together for lunch once in a while to celebrate their combined love of 'their dog'. I understand this completely because Monkey Dog and I are in love. And this is why . . . .

My villa borders the Sacred Monkey Forest in Ubud. On my very first day, I watched, aghast, as about fifty monkeys moved through, spreading themselves all over the patio, the back wall and the shrine.

They jumped all over the roof, shimmied down the pipes, pressed their squashed faces against the windows, and dive bombed from the trees into the pond. "OMG, these guys own the joint!" I thought.

Tiny babies hung onto the bellies of their mums, teenagers swam in the pond, dunking each other. The King, big balls swinging, strutted around being the boss. Every now and then, he'd lift the tail of one of his concubines, climb on and mate her. All two seconds worth.

It was like I was given a front row seat to some bizarre community theatre. It was fascinating and frightening all at once.

My fear gave way to indignation when one grabbed a cushion I'd left outside on the bench. I leapt outside, screaming like a banshee and waving my arms.

He just sat there, unmoved, and held on tight. "Oh God! Now what?" I mustered up my courage, grabbing the nearest thing, a bamboo ladder, shoving it towards him.

But instead of dropping his treasure and running, he lunged for me, screeching loudly, exposing big yellow teeth that glistened menacingly in the light.

I did what came naturally. I dropped the ladder and ran, slamming the glass sliding doors together just a fraction of a second before he threw himself at the door. "Where's the key?" I yelled to no one. Oh shit, it's on the outside instead of the inside.

Three times he body-slammed into the glass sliding doors, our eyes locking as I desperately held the doors shut. Finally tiring of the game, he picked up 'his' purple pillow and disappeared into the forest.

At this stage I was a shaking mess. Locking the door securely, I lay down on the bed, feeling like a drop kick for my obvious ineptitude, shaking from primordial fear.

So I did what I learned to do at the women's group in Byron Bay. I laid down, took a deep breath and focussed on my feet, feeling the energy slowly course through them into my legs through my solar plexus and my entire body to the crown of my head.

Five minutes later, I was calm once again.

I then called on the Divine Mothers and the Angels for help. I did not want to leave this beautiful jungle home with its colourful birds and butterflies, huge geckos and light-footed squirrels.

I did not want to leave its cascading ravine and soothing water sounds. Nor its ancient trees, dripping with vines.

I so loved it here. "I've found paradise and now I have to leave?" I asked.

I had barely finished my prayer when Monkey Dog appeared, snarling and barking at the monkeys on the porch, lunging for them as they scattered.

The mums and kids took to the vines and hid themselves in the trees but some of the alpha males stayed around for the game. Dog barking and snapping at their tails and back legs till the monkeys found spots just out of reach on the old stone fence that bordered the ravine.

One even lunged for Monkey Dog as he was chasing another but backed off when the dog whipped around and bit him. That did it. They left, in a flurry of screeches.

Phew! Finally, with all 50 or so monkeys gone, a very satisfied dog came and introduced himself to me, nuzzling my hand and my face. It was love, and I had decided to stay.

The purpose of that sweet story is to highlight two very simple and effective (and even miraculous!) techniques I've learned to use.

The grounding technique that calmed me after my crazy monkey experience, I use daily. It helps me stay present and brings awareness and clarity.

Often you'll find me sitting with my feet flat on the floor, at a meeting, or over dinner, or painting art or just whenever I remember. By focusing on the soles of my feet and how they meet the ground, I draw in the grounded energy.

I am always amazed at how quickly this process works. It expands the space around my thoughts, calms me and allows me to be aware of my surroundings, body sensations and thoughts.

I experiment with this technique a lot and have found that I can simultaneously focus on the energy at my feet and paint, or talk or drive at the same time . . . and there is a heightened sense of awareness happening and a sweetness: a kind of bliss.

If you were to ask me what the most effective and easiest path to mindfulness is, and what the most powerful tool to assist you to become aware/conscious is, this is what I would suggest.

It's like the magic wand of awareness. The more you try it, the more expansive your awareness becomes.

You'll find more detailed info on grounding in the Meditation and Mindfulness chapter of this book because it's an intrinsic part of mindfulness and it's the first stage of every meditation process.

Grounding is also particularly useful when caught in an overwhelming emotional charge.

I often combine this with deep circular breathing, where I slowly fill my lungs starting at the belly, lifting it up to the chest, fully filling my lungs and then slowly exhaling . . . all the while feeling the energy coming through my feet.

Sometimes you don't have the luxury of lying down and centering yourself, you're on your feet and have to deal with something or someone. It works anywhere, anytime.

Next time something has been triggered in you and you suddenly feel all anxious and contracted, try using this grounding technique.

As for asking the Angels (or Divine Mothers or Universal Energy or God/Goddess or whatever fits right for you) for support, help or guidance, this never came easy for me when I first started . . . mainly because I didn't believe in Angels or even God, for that matter. Certainly not in the God the nuns portrayed to me in primary school.

That being said, over the years I've become more comfortable with talking to a higher power and asking for guidance. I have a friend who summons up Yoda! It doesn't matter which form it takes . . . it's only important that you ask.

Generally, I do this at night before I go to sleep and often the solution pops into my mind the instant I wake up, or I find that during that week I am drawn to someone or something that assists me in what I've asked for.

Many of you already pray . . . but does it come out all needy and whiney or fearful and disempowered? Better to ground yourself first, and then from that place of centredness, ask for support.

You see the difference? You aren't going to God (or whoever you pray to or get guidance from) like a two year old having a tantrum, you are asking from a calm place.

You have already displayed some willingness on your part to do your bit by being grounded and open to support.

You are already moving in the direction of peace and open to receiving.

Chapter Two:
Trauma Therap

The good thing about early trauma (whether you know you've been traumatised or not) is that it can sometimes create an urge to grow.

I only found out I was traumatized as a new born when I was 56 (in 2014). I had no idea that I'd been all alone in a glass cage without being held by my mum for two whole weeks until I had that experience in the women's circle.

My mum hadn't told me. So how did I come to find out, over half a century later, in the middle of a circle of women?

First, let me tell you what a women's circle is. There are all kinds of women's circles, some with rituals, some with prayer, some are meditation groups, some are Wicca women circles, some are groups of women who come together because they share a common issue.

This women's circle was for those women interested in Truth . . . those who endeavour to be mindful.

It was for those who had tasted the vastness at the core of their being from which everything arises. For those who had realised that this core is truly who they are . . . more than their thoughts and their bodies.

These women had spent many months or years at Satsangs (more on this later).

Up to a dozen of us gathered together once a week, not to chatter or gossip or even share highs and lows, but mostly to sit, as a group, in the stillness of who we are. We did talk, but only to acknowledge something that was happening for us in that moment.

We didn't attach long-winded stories to what caused the feelings that came, we simply touched briefly on the fact that something was moving through us. This would be silently acknowledged by the others in the circle and held like a quiet caress in consciousness.

Some of the women in this group have had experience with somatic trauma therapy. Somatic therapy is a body awareness approach to healing trauma.

I have seen and experienced amazing healings and life-changing transformations in this circle. It's a place where we consciously connect through our bodies to release old harmful patterns and pain.

It's a kind of free flowing mixture of grounding, mindfulness, meditation, somatic therapy and love.

Back to the present, when our guide Meike looked at me unswervingly and uttered the words 'I see you Mel', my 'baby' experience was triggered. I had no idea what it was that unexpectedly had me in a silent frozen grip.

Suddenly I was aware of this intense loneliness, this outrageous grief. In the next moment, I was just a blubbering mess, totally immersed in my infant experience and oh so fortunate to have the arms of a loving woman around me to help me internalise and complete something that had remained incomplete inside me for 56 years.

The other women in the circle who held the space while I was going through my experience told me later that my fists were all balled up and my feet curled, just like a baby.

I fully re-lived my baby experience . . . only this time, I was seen, heard and held so that I could be fully healed.

This remarkable process prompted a phone call to my mother that night. I had already known I barely survived and put in a humidicrib straight after I was born. But until this phone call, I didn't realise that she was not allowed to hold me for over two weeks. Bam! It all came together.

Much research has been done regarding the importance of touch for infants. So it doesn't take a genius to imagine how it is for a baby who is left on her own straight after birth without knowing the sweet and reassuring arms of her mother.

The point I'm making is that many of us have experienced some trauma that gets locked in our cells and our nervous system and many of us have no idea that we have been traumatised. But we often have a common thread weaving through our lives . . . our motivation for personal growth.

I had a blessed childhood, full of love and support. And yet, even with such a great foundation, I was still always searching for answers, joining personal growth groups, sitting in Satsangs with spiritual teachers and even dabbling with drugs . . . all in an effort to answer a question many have struggled with— "What's it all about?".

I was trying to find the meaning of life, to find meaning in myself. I wanted to live a life of love and fulfilment . . . and to be at peace.

My first foray into self-discovery was in Cairns, Qld. I was 22 years old.

A good friend of mine, named Desley, was a psychologist there. We met through my boyfriend Michael, who was a DJ at the local radio station. Desley had a spot on the radio too—she had a way of telling stories about herself and her experiences that totally engaged people.

She was the first professional woman I knew who used the 'F' word and I think she stood out to me because of that. Mostly because you don't expect it from a woman in her field of work but also because she was so comfortable with herself, she didn't care what anyone else thought about her.

At the time, I rarely swore but I loved and idolised her. Wanted to be like her.

Even though I always exuded confidence, truthfully I was terrified of being in the spotlight; I was terrified of really being seen.

It's strange because, by nature, I'm quite exuberant. I've been called optimistic, confident and fun and told that people warm to me. That being said, put me in the spotlight among people I don't know and I would be a shaking mess.

Michael and I owned a restaurant in Cairns at the time. Good God, talk about working our arses off!

Word of advice here: never get into the hospitality industry unless you have a big stash of money to employ loads of people right from the start and give yourself some time off. But we were young and stupid and thought we could work hard and do the work of many by ourselves.

We were totally consumed with the business, starting at 8 am and working well past midnight seven days a week. It was a nightmare.

About a year into it, I just couldn't face it anymore. So Michael suggested I take a break and visit my family and friends in Perth, WA for a week.

Five days into my holiday, I got a phone call from him. The restaurant had burnt to the ground . . . something to do with a gas burner being left on. Almost everything we owned destroyed.

I came back . . . to no home. We had lived in the flat below the restaurant and that was a charred mess. We were devastated. Financially and emotionally crippled.

It was at this time that I asked Desley if there was some sort of workshop I could attend that would help me through this rough patch. And so I attended my first personal growth workshop.

There were about 20 people, many of them professionals in the psychology field. The facilitator was a Gestalt therapy expert. What's wonderful about workshops is that everyone gets to work on their stuff, professionals and laymen alike.

One at a time, the facilitator assisted people with their issues. Big teddy bears were brought out which were used as replacements for those in our lives we might have issues with or couldn't normally speak to.

We'd talk to the teddies as if they were our husbands, our children, our boss or our parents. Pillows were brought out for people with anger issues who needed something to slam to express their anger and frustration.

I watched and listened intently, amazed at the ease with which those in the profession expressed themselves via these teddies and pillows. I guess they had some practice!

Suddenly it was my turn and I froze. She, who generally never has much trouble expressing herself, froze like rabbit in the headlights. I attempted to mumble something and stopped.

My heart was pumping much too fast, adrenaline was coursing through my veins like a river of hot lava. Spiky heat formed streams of sweat under my arms and down my face as I felt all eyes and ears on me.

I was in the spotlight, in a room full of strangers and couldn't speak.

Desley, bless her, jumped in and spoke for me. Expressing all my anguish at the loss of my business, the fears I had that Michael may have torched it (turns out he didn't) because of my inability to cope with the intense workload and pressure, the self-loathing I had because of my failure to step up to the plate!

All the things I had shared with her over tea and tears at her home only days before . . . and she said it so truly! It was as if I had said it myself. So there was a healing of sorts in that for me.

But what wasn't healed, what continued to plague me for decades, was my inability to work through my traumas, my knee-jerk response of frozenness in the thick of trauma.

You see, Gestalt psychology, while more cathartic than many forms of psych treatment, still works on the premise that it's a mind-based problem. Working on the mind brings understanding, sure . . . . But as I learned later, understanding is a shiny but worthless prize.

It does nothing to release the trauma locked in the body, does nothing about that knee-jerk nervous system response when the old trauma has been triggered.

The brain usually deals with things with the cortex part of the brain. But fight, flight or freeze issues get dealt with by the reptilian brain at the back and bottom of the cortex.

The cortex, as you may know, has left and right sides to it that 'talk' to each other. But the reptilian brain doesn't 'talk' to the cortex. That's why understanding is a false prize.

No matter what psychotherapy you generally do or how much you understand what the problem is, if it's trauma-related it simply gets locked into your nervous system waiting to be triggered.

This cell/nervous system memory can be triggered into fight, flight or freeze with even the slightest hint of a situation.

People who have bad car accidents can often break out in a sweat years later when they see a car coming from a similar angle towards them. Their nervous system just got triggered.

That's why many people suffer from panic attacks; it's a trigger from an old trauma. No amount of understanding or mind-based therapy eliminates it. It can't be worked out with understanding.

What is needed for these situations is a body-centered approach that integrates a person's physical body into the therapy.

Had I not experienced the release that somatic trauma therapy brought me that day in the women's circle, I know I'd still freeze up when speaking in public. I don't suffer from that anymore. I'd also still be needy . . . and I'm not that anymore either.

I want to share another story about my experience with this somatic therapy. I cannot tell you the details of the trauma because I don't want people second-guessing who was involved. Everyone is entitled to his or her privacy and I respect that.

Suffice to say that I was told the most shocking news that involved people I loved who had betrayed me. While I was so glad that I was finally told, as it confirmed all those intuitive, gnawing, gut-level feelings I had about something being 'off' at the time, to hear this news a few years later completely shocked and hurt me to the core.

Fortunately for me, I took it to the women's circle. Remember, this isn't about talking at length about your issues and getting agreement from the auxiliary about how terrible it is, how bad the perpetrators are or how sorry everyone is for you.

This is about being 'held' in a sacred space with loving and self-aware women and getting some guidance in dealing with it.

So I bottom-lined the scenario into a couple of sentences, feeling the emotions come up as I spat out the words. Meike held me in her gaze and asked me to just shift my attention to a part of my body.

For a minute or so I did . . . . It felt like I had a bit more space to breathe . . . until the thoughts and feelings came up again and were almost to that point of overwhelming me.

Meike again directed my attention back to my body. We did this back and forth for about an hour, maybe more, maybe less . . . I don't know because there was no 'time' for me in that place, in that space.

I do know that the feelings of emotion were becoming lighter and less charged until . . . they were simply not there anymore. Even more astounding is that *they never came back.*

Truly, it was nothing short of a miracle. This betrayal and the issues surrounding it was something that could have seriously fucked me up for years to come and yet, here I am, totally free of any emotional charge about it.

Some of my best friends were skeptical, watching me closely in the following months, believing that I could be in denial, that I'd buried the trauma. How could I possibly be ok so quickly after the shock of such a betrayal?

But in time, they too saw that I was indeed free. So free that I was able to hop on a plane and speak to that person, and was able to tell them I knew about what happened and that I forgave them—that I loved them.

This would have been impossible had I not truly been free.

Why was I able to move through this trauma without so much as a scratch? To me it's the stuff of miracles.

I'm absolutely sure it's to do with the way I was being redirected to my body and its sensations whenever I was almost at the point of overwhelm.

Perhaps the nervous system was able to form a 'new groove'. Instead of the triggering thought leading straight to emotional break down, my attention was directed to my body, slowing the nervous system process down and eventually forming a new groove, a new response that led to spaciousness instead of knee-jerk pain.

All I really know is that it worked. I was free.

Trauma is inevitable in our lives. We deal with it in all kinds of ways. Chances are that something trauma-inducing happened to all of us as we were growing up.

It's also very likely your parents didn't say to you "Just take a breath and be with that feeling, just feel where in your body you're holding this fear." Nope. With the very best of intentions, our parents sought to make us strong by teaching us to ignore fear and telling us to be a "big boy or girl."

We were taught to override our fears, not to take the time to be with them and the sensations in the body. Inevitably, we are left with many unresolved traumas that haven't been integrated and resolved, and they come back to bite us whenever they get triggered.

It's not too late to be with them now though. As adults, we have both the suppressed traumas triggering us or very real in-the-moment traumas to deal with and if we could just let ourselves be with the sensations, we are taking very huge leaps in our growth.

It's clear to me that trauma lives in the body. So on a journey of healing trauma it makes sense to come back to the body. The nature of trauma disassociates us from the body.

Body dissociation is a survival mechanism. It is a strong feeling of detachment from the body, often described as a feeling of emotional numbness.

This is where the idea of safety in the body is key.

If the body is a place of anxiety or terror, how do we begin to come back to the body to find safety without further traumatizing ourselves?

By becoming aware of our body sensations.

If you've had a lot of trauma in your life, it can be difficult to even start. So first, work on the little things, and as the little things integrate, the body starts to trust . . . . These little things are actually monumental shifts.

Get assistance with a somatic therapist you feel safe with. We need to feel that we're not alone with the boogieman. We need to know that there is someone there to hold our hand.

Be willing to take that first step. Have the willingness to move in the direction of the trauma, be willing to allow the vulnerability. I'm not saying throwing ourselves head first into the pit, but with little increments at a time.

For those of you interested in researching this kind of therapy, Dr. Peter Levine's Somatic Experiencing site is www.somaticexperiencing.com.

If you suffer from panic attacks or get 'frozen' or know you are over reacting to certain things but can't seem to help it, or are disassociating and cutting off in any way, these body-centered therapies are immensely valuable.

I have such heartfelt gratitude to the pioneers of this therapy, because without them and those who facilitate this work I would not be free.

suffering that we are reluctant to let it go.

Just wait and see the next time the shit hits the fan in your life and watch how the mind loves a drama. How attached it gets to the suffering. So much so that the last thing on earth you want to do is think of things to be grateful for.

The mind is so naughty like that. It just gets fixated on the suffering . . . like that weird hobbit character obsessing over that ring. It LIKES to suffer.

And then it likes to tell stories to other people about the suffering. It's relentless. It doesn't want to be grateful, it wants to complain, damn it!

My suggestion here is don't let it have its way. When you go to bed with dark thoughts, you are doing yourself a monumental disservice. You are, in effect, drawing more darkness towards you.

It's more important than ever to mentally run through the list of things to be grateful for at these times. It's also harder than ever to find things to be grateful for. But you'll find them.

I find it easiest to just start with the simple things . . . like the bed I'm lying in, the food I had for dinner, the clothes I wear, or the shower I took.

You know how lucky we are to have these things in our lives that we take for granted? So start with the little things and you'll find they will lead to other things to be grateful for.

Oh . . . and one other thing: don't only *think* about things to be grateful for, let your heart *feel* what that gratitude brings. Without involving your heart, all you're doing is ticking off a list. It has no impact.

If you were grateful for the shower you had that day, just for a moment, feel what that shower felt like, smell that beautiful new soap you bought. Enjoy reliving the feeling of the way the warm water eases the tension in your neck, the freshness you feel, the aliveness.

This brings you to your heart, to TRULY feel grateful. Gratitude felt from the heart will increase your joy, improve your relationships and bring more of the good stuff into your life.

Just do it. Especially when you don't want to . . . just do it.

Chapter Four:
Your Vibe Attracts
Your Tribe

Going solo to restaurants almost anywhere in the world can be a solitary affair . . . but not in Ubud. It's alive with people who love to connect.

I can walk into any restaurant, scout the joint for people who look like they are having a good time or people dining alone who look like they could do with some company and ask if I can join them. Not one person has hesitated, not one has said no.

Some nights I'm happy to just sit alone, soaking up the atmosphere, eating my meal slowly, savouring every bite. Just being totally present with the experience.

The night I met Melati was one of those nights. The Bali Bohemia in a little village of Nyuh Kuning five minutes from Ubud was such a find! It's run by a Palestinian and French couple who might just be the coolest people in Ubud.

Their restaurant reflected their personalities: bright and full of colour. There were hand painted murals covering the walls and multi-coloured cushions scattered over intricately carved Balinese benches. There were flowers and candles adorning tables and huge swaths of colourful fabric billowing from ceilings.

I had just finished a yummy crispy Tempe with satay sauce, polished off a strawberry daiquiri and was watching the band just in front of me set up their array of interesting instruments, which included a sitar, flute, tabla, electric guitar and a lute. The place was rapidly filling up with people coming to watch and listen.

Since I was sitting alone at the table closest to the band, I was just about to tell the waitress to offer the remaining seats to whoever wanted a seat when a woman came up to me.

Her eyes danced playfully behind her glasses and her long platinum hair fell over a dress printed with colourful flowers mimicking the frangipani tucked behind her ear.

With an unmistakeable Aussie accent, she chirped, "Would you mind if our little group join you?" Well, it was like I'd found a long lost sister, the way we hit it off that night.

There's a saying "your vibe attracts your tribe" and that rang true for me this night. Turns out she had lived in my much loved tiny country town of Denmark, WA a few years after I had left to live in Byron Bay. What are the odds?

We had some of the same friends. Yes, really. We even did the same personal growth workshop. She squealed when I told her about doing Inward Adventures in the eighties. "OMG, I did one too!" she said.

Heartfelt sharing of stories and much laughter later, we exchanged phone numbers and promised to connect again soon.

What I'm suggesting with this story is that we attract those who are like us. This can work against you if you're a Negative Nancy because guess what? You'll attract negativity. You'll attract people who complain a lot, people who blame a lot. So work on that vibe baby!

Don't worry, by the time you finish this book and start to put some of the suggestions into practice, you too will be a bright shining light, attracting good people and experiences into your life.

Chapter Five: Personal Growth Workshops

I was in my late 20's hanging out with my good friend Macca in the mid 80's, when he suggested Inward Adventure to me.

Macca and I have loved each other forever, over many lives if there is such a thing. He is a big bear of a man with a heart to match.

His mate, Colin, had been running these personal growth workshops for many years. So Macca took me along with him to an introduction night and three hours of Charismatic Colin later I was hooked.

This guy totally owned the floor. "There's nothing back there worth turning your head for," he announced, acting it out with a flick of his head and a wave of his arm.

He was acting out 'past' and 'future'. Running to one side of the room saying "when I have that promotion I want, then I'll be happy", then running to the other side bemoaning "if only she hadn't left, me, I was so happy then".

Backwards and forwards, backwards and forwards, example after example . . . till he stopped dead in the centre of the room and silently looked around the room. "The past and future are only thoughts, not real at all and yet we are living them . . . right now", he said.

There were all kinds of amazing stories with huge impacts, backed up by masterful acting. It struck the core of my being that day.

A week later I did the four-day Inward Adventure and it changed my life forever. Everything I had thought was real had been turned on its head.

I realised that I'd been limited by thoughts and beliefs my whole life and miraculously, after only four days at an

Inward Adventure, I felt free. I totally 'got' that I was not my thoughts, that my beliefs were simply handed over to me from years of conditioning.

It was my first taste of Truth and a really significant stepping stone into conscious awareness.

It's decades ago so I'm a bit hazy on the details and the processes I went through. I do remember sitting, for what seemed like hours, with my head in a bucket shouting out "I don't need to compete to be loved!"

I also remember a very simple heart-opening process that involved sitting in front of a perfect stranger and just looking into each other's eyes and maintaining eye contact for 30 minutes.

At first it was rather disconcerting being eye-to-eye with someone I didn't know. But after a while, as we stared into each other's eyes, I started to relax, and felt a connection growing.

I began to recognise myself in those eyes. Then the tears flowed, my heart sang and joy bubbled up inside me. It was such an awesome experience, just sitting there looking into someone else's eyes.

Another thing I will never forget is dancing naked and wild with a bunch of naked others. I can't tell you how freeing that was once I'd gotten over my shyness and inhibitions.

Our bodies are beautiful, in each of their varied forms and yet we are so caught up in societal norms that often we become ashamed of our bodies. There's nothing quite like naked dancing to push those boundaries and find acceptance and love for our physical form.

Besides that, it's such fun dancing naked!

There were also videos . . . the old series "Monkey", the Harold and Maud movie, The Circle of Iron with David Carradine, as well as videos of Osho talking about religion.

I also remember Colin dragging out a drawer full of tapes (back in the day when digital data wasn't around) and using the tapes as an example of our conditioned minds.

Above all though, I remember a beautiful process of Blessing and Freeing of all those we had issues with.

Such a simple process in forgiveness, where you hold that person in your mind and as you bless them, your hands come together in prayer, lips touch your fingertips. Then you free them in a glorious opening of your arms to the sky.

"I bless you (hands in prayer) and I free you (hands open and wide above your head)." Doing this over and over again for at least five minutes every day can bring you to bliss.

The bliss of forgiveness.

The bliss of creating space in your heart where hardness once lived.

Lastly, there were the amazing meditations. There was a guided meditation that took us through levels of experience through imagination and brought such peace.

Guided meditations are more like being taken on a little inner adventure, where, directed by the dialogue, you use your imagination to come to peaceful, loving and healing spaces.

But what really impressed me were the Osho meditations that involved lots of movement first, like shaking our bodies and acting out and dancing . . . till finally we lay down to silence.

I'd never been able to meditate before that, certainly it never brought me peace. It just accentuated how busy my mind was. But doing those Osho active meditations, which involved stages of movements first—sometimes intense and physical—followed by a period of silence, was the first time I'd ever known stillness.

Osho, the twentieth century Indian mystic, created several active meditation techniques to help the contemporary seeker reach an experience of meditation, self-observation and inner stillness with great ease and speed.

These meditations are practiced by millions of people all over the world today. There are two I highly recommend; the first is the Osho Kundalini meditation, which is a good one for beginners and later on, try the Osho Dynamic meditation, which is much more intense and physically exerting but also much more powerful.

I will also never forget some of the "Ruthless Rules of Reality" that were stuck on the wall:

> You Create Your Own Reality
>
> Ain't No Such Thing As A Free Lunch.

What You Addictively Demand, You Emotionally Repel.

Declaration = Liberation

Argue For Your Limitations . . . and Sure Enough, They're Yours!

Understanding Is the Booby Prize

Image Is a Dream, Beauty Is Real

Are Your Resentments Worth More Than Your Freedom?

Though they are only one-liners, they are very profound teachings and have stuck with me as pointers for decades.

Inward Adventure no longer runs, as Colin has retired now, but there are all kinds of personal growth workshops available these days. Do some research, ask around, get recommendations and GO FOR IT! These kind of groups help kick start your liberation.

Chapter Six:
Opting out of
Mainstream Media

One of the many consequences of doing such a powerful personal transformation workshop was that I stopped watching television. All this make-believe stuff no longer held my interest when reality was so much more compelling.

Not only that, I also realized that mainstream media has tremendous power in setting cultural guidelines and in shaping political discourse. It's biased in favour of who owns the station and which political shoulders are being rubbed. So I didn't want to subject myself to the bullshit anymore.

Fast forward 30 years and I'm still not watching TV, but I'm finding myself in front of Facebook every day and I started to feel myself being dragged into the stories that friends are posting.

Many of them expressed concerns over government issues like the proposed banning of peaceful protests, the proposed Internet censorship, Monsanto's grip on our food production and the toxic chemicals they use on our food, the proposed mandatory adult vaccinations, the hard stand on refugees, etc., etc.

The list of concerns was large and these concerns spilled into my world every day on Facebook and online.

I watched myself become anxious and angry as I started to get on the bandwagon of signing every petition against these issues. However, the more I signed, the more I received emails asking me to assist with another cause. More and more of the 'wrongs' I needed to help get 'right'. And all the while, my buttons were being pressed.

Bizarrely, it felt like I was becoming part of the problem because how on earth do we help change things for the better when we come from a place of fear or anger?

And so one day, when I was going to a women's gathering, I brought this subject up. A friend of mine, Cushla Lovejoy, gave us a sound healing. She also called in the Divine Mothers and spoke about whatever it was that was troubling us.

So on this day, I asked the Divine Mothers for a solution to my getting caught up every time I see a Facebook post about some injustice. Below is the answer I was given.

"We want you to understand that you have the power to make a difference and be a part of the change you want to see, and we want you to know that these issues are best dealt with on an energetic level.

Your complaints, your fears, your constant talking in circles about issues, be they personal, national or global, do not serve yourself or the world. Rather, we suggest that the best course of action is on an energetic level and we are strongly suggesting you do the following:

Imagine yourself in a blue room. See those you have issues with, be they government heads or people you know, in the room with you.

Speak to them from your heart about your concerns and imagine them to be attentive listeners.

Know that in this room, your communication is heard and imagine them being very receptive and engaging in conversation with you and attempting to come up with the best solutions for everyone's highest good.

We thank you for your energetic contributions and we promise you that there will be great outcomes as a result."

This communication really struck a chord with me because I knew in my gut that I wasn't doing the world or myself any favours by getting sucked into stories on the Internet. I know that feeling anxious and angry does not serve me or others.

Since receiving this guidance I have been playing in my blue room a lot with both personal and global issues. It's difficult to tell you whether my blue room work is having an effect on global issues but I'm happy with the wondrous effect it's having on a more personal level.

I no longer feel angry or anxious every time I see a Facebook post on some issue that used to send me into a mini-spin. I no longer buy into these stories. I simply send love and move along.

Chapter Seven: Satsang

I've mentioned Satsang a few times so far in this book. So what is it? Satsang is a Sanskrit word meaning "meeting in highest truth".

What this means in a more familiar way for many people, since there are Satsangs held all over the world, is a gathering of people coming together to discover the truth about who they really are.

There is usually a spiritual teacher, someone who has gone beyond the limitations of the mind, who leads the dialogue with the others. This dialogue can often be interspersed with deep silence.

Now, some of my more conservative, intellectual friends make fun of my going to these meetings. They deem them as new age mumbo jumbo. And yet, they have never gone to experience a Satsang for themselves so how on Earth can they possibly know?

Admittedly, I too was a bit skeptical the first time I heard about them, but I am inherently curious and was keen to see what it was all about.

My first Satsang was with Gangaji when I was around 40. She is an American teacher or guru who regularly gives Satsangs around the globe. She is said to have attained self-realization in 1990 after an encounter with Poonjaji, a disciple of Ramana Maharshi, who sent her back to the West to teach.

I'd seen some videos of her holding Satsangs before and had resonated with what she was saying.

So when I heard she was coming to Denmark, Western Australia where I lived, I knew I had to go. What also attracted me to going was that she is a woman and I'd never heard of a female spiritual teacher before.

Now, all these years later, I cannot remember a thing she said but I remember clearly how my heart felt. Full and overflowing!

And lo and behold, without any effort, my mind was totally silent and calm. Not every time I went though, just the once. But once was enough for me to see there was something here I wanted to explore.

Tomas Stubbs explains what happens at Satsangs beautifully.

"True Satsang is a meeting in support of Awakening, for Awakening to arise not just in the time of the meeting but supporting any opening which is already happening for those that come.

So, true Satsang requires as much from those that attend as from the one who gives and facilitates it. What makes the difference between a normal meeting and Satsang is the intention of Awakening with Presence anchored.

The role of the Satsang giver is to be that anchor for Awareness which is what happens when someone awakens, Presence anchors itself. Without that anchor of Presence, which really is the holding of the space, there can be no Satsang, it would just be sitting in a group, maybe talking, maybe a debate.

We are fortunate these days that even in a very small group there is likely to be a couple or more anchors for Presence in any Satsang—those who can hold that space."

Of course, when I was new to Satsang, I didn't know what to expect or that the person holding the group in Presence can actually have an influence in bringing me to Presence.

What I did learn from experience was that there were moments there while I was listening to the discourse where I felt like I could breathe through my mind.

I know how silly that sounds, but it's the closest I can get to describing the experience. Suddenly, the noise in my mind would cease.

There was so much space and yet, I was acutely conscious of everything. Going to Satsangs was the first time I had experienced this.

In my personal journey, Meike was that "anchor of Presence" within the women's circle. Isaac Shapiro, her partner, was another. Meike and Isaac hold Satsangs and retreats together.

While I have gone to Satsangs held by many different people, the sweetest and most powerful clarity and presence comes to me with these two yummy ones. It's a very personal thing really. There will always be some people that you resonate with more than others.

Meike and Isaac are based in Byron Bay, Australia but also travel around Australia and the world together holding Satsang and retreats.

In this digital age, we are also very fortunate to have videos of live Satsangs from people all over the globe. I would recommend both Mooji and Adyashanti if you want to get a taste of Satsang via the Internet.

For those of you with a christian background, I'd definitely recommend checking out Francis Bennett. Once a monk at a monastery, he now holds Satsangs (although he doesn't call them that, he simply calls them Meetings in Truth) in the U.S.A. and in various parts of the world. He is also starting an online 'School For Contemplative Living'. This virtual school will be a way for people to access Francis' teachings and to engage in one on one contact, without necessarily committing to the time and expense of travelling to a retreat.

There is also a great site called Buddha at the Gas Pump where the host and insightful interviewer, Rick Archer, has videos of hundreds of interviews with people from all walks of life who have experienced Awakening.

Chapter Eight: Sisterhood (and Brotherhood)

"Whoo hoooo Mellllllleeeeeee" echoed around me as Melati arrived to pick me up.

I had phoned her right after another harrowing experience with Bully Monkey. Monkey Dog and I were inside the villa, sharing breakfast, when suddenly out of nowhere, Bully Monkey pounced on the glass door.

"BOOOF!" slammed the monkey; "WOOF WOOF" went Monkey Dog. BOOF! WOOF! BOOF! WOOF! Monkey Dog was going off!

He was barking and snarling as Bully Monkey continued to bash into the door with the full force of his weight. Their faces and gnarling teeth were only millimetres apart between the glass.

"Any second now that glass is gonna break," I thought. "Oh sweet Mother, where is my slingshot????" Adrenalin coursed through me, pushing me into action.

Ignoring the shaking of my hands, I grabbed the sling shot from my bedside table, rushed to the glass and put on my Fierce Face, and the monkey and I locked eyes.

I was only a meter away from him, dangling the sling in front of his eyes. No stone attached of course . . . . I'd break the bloody window and the show would be over. But did Bully Monkey know that?

Feet shoulder length apart, knees slightly bent, taking a deep breath, feeling the chi power running through me . . . . I pulled back hard on the sling and . . . "OMG, it worked!"

Bully Monkey backed off, jumped onto the wall, threw himself onto a swinging vine and disappeared into the Sacred Forest.

Monkey Dog relaxed into a laying position and once again, I found myself lying on the bed, going through the centring motions. When the tremor had left my body, I phoned Melati and ask her if she wanted to help me find a new place to stay. "I have an idea", she said. "I'll pick you up and we'll talk over lunch".

It was really only in my older years that I came to realise the importance of hanging out with women. Perhaps that's because in those "hormonal" years I was so obsessed with men.

Besides which, in my teens, twenties and even thirties, I found most women of my age to be a bit silly really. Many spent time gossiping and comparing and being total bitches. I much preferred hanging out with men in those years.

It was only after I started doing personal growth work and meeting women who were interested in what made them tick, who, like me, knew that there must be more to life than what the magazines and TV shows that society put out there as normal and have something to aspire to.

The thing about meeting women who you really connect with, women with honour and heart, women with a passion for the Truth, is that you can speak about anything and be exactly who you are without being judged.

That means you aren't being subtly coerced into feeling guilt or shame. It means that you can allow yourself to put it all out there to see and to experience without judgment from others or yourself!

When others hold that space for you to be authentic, it gives you the space to step back from yourself and not take yourself so seriously

When they acknowledge you, when they really hear you, when they see you just as you are, it helps you to see your own behavior; your trickiness, your games, your hurts, and your darker side from a place of vastness and truth.

The seeing itself is all that is required . . . no need to do anything about it. Just having seen things as they are without personalizing it is enough for the shadow to lose its power and momentum.

I have a few of these gorgeous women in my life back in Australia. We get together for impromptu meals . . . sharing food, wine and ourselves.

We listen, we sooth, we encourage, we hug, we laugh, we cry, we sing, we dance, we just be together and celebrate our connection.

I'd only met Melati a few days earlier but knew already that she was one of those people who I could totally relax and be myself with. I could drop her right there at our women's gathering in Australia and she'd fit right in.

So, I'm sitting here at Melati's beautiful villa, enjoying the cool breeze bringing the scent of frangipani, drinking a cold Bintang, when she suggests the solution to my monkey problem.

She told me that one of her bungalows on the property had become available and that I should become her neighbour! I accepted with glee.

I knew I'd met a soul sister right then and there. She and I spent many beautiful, honest, straight talking, heart sharing, laughter and tear filled months together.

And so, I encourage you women to meet with other women. And I also urge you men to meet with other men. There is much more to life when you share yourself as you are, with nothing hidden.

You'll know who your soul brothers and soul sisters are by their unabashed honesty and in the way they share themselves. They don't have an inner adjudicator, weighing up what to say, how much to share. They just let rip.

They also stop and listen, really listen, so that you actually feel heard. They don't offer advice so much as offer a safe place for others to share what's going on.

So speak up. Share yourself. Be yourself. Your brothers and sisters will recognise you and you will form important lifelong connections.

Chapter Nine: Meditation and Mindfulness

The dogs in Bali are so different from Western dogs. Did you know that they are allowed to roam the streets at any time, day or night? Not like in the Western world at all.

I wonder whether it's this freedom the Bali dogs have that makes them so different. They have such free spirits. They don't bother trying to please you like the dogs we have. In fact, they are more like cats in this way since they live more for themselves than for others.

They are also more relaxed, taking their own good time about things. When you drive towards a dog lying on the road in Bali, he doesn't scatter and run away, he limbers up slowly to his feet and nonchalantly makes his way to the sidewalk.

In fact, Bali dogs have similar qualities to meditators. Which leads me to the crux of this book. Meditators are more relaxed. They also tend to be free spirits. Why? Well that's because they are not governed and controlled by their thoughts.

You see, mindfulness and meditation are the only ways of retrieving reality from the dream world most people are lost in. This can be difficult sometimes because the dream is so encompassing.

What do I mean about this dream? It's the life of thought. It's the belief that you are your thoughts. It's the constant identification with thought.

Meditation and mindfulness give those thoughts some space.

In essence, we need not awaken *from* the dream but *to* the dream. In lucid dreaming, you wake up inside a dream, realize it is a dream, and then continue the dream with this understanding.

It's possible that meditation and mindfulness can lead to awakening in that it allows us to see through the illusion of separation, described by Leo Hartong as "lucid living", explaining that "it is not you waking up *from* the dream of life, but the impersonal awakening *to* the dream of life".

For those who are beginners on the path and have no idea what I'm going on about, let me paint you a picture.

Imagine a blue sky . . . a beautiful, vast and expansive blue that goes on forever. Now imagine a few clouds drifting through the sky . . . then add a few more . . . . Keep doing so until the sky is covered with clouds.

Then, as in real life, imagine the clouds breaking up and disappearing, revealing the blue sky. The clouds come and go while the sky is ever present.

What I am alluding to here is that YOU are the sky, the ever present being, while the clouds are the thoughts that come and go. You are not your thoughts; you are the space they occupy.

Just stop and look for yourself.

The best way to look is by quieting the voice in your head through meditation. You know that voice I'm talking about. It goes on and on about all kinds of useless crap.

It can be so noisy and so unrelenting sometimes that it drives you bonkers. Now imagine that the voice inside your head stops. Just stops.

Suddenly, it's so exquisitely quiet.

This can happen through meditation. I won't guarantee that it will happen instantly, or even that it will happen at all, because this isn't the goal. TRYING to stop the mind is like trying to stop the wind. But meditation helps to soften the din.

It gives you some respite from the barrage, slowing your thoughts down enough to notice who it is that sees these thoughts.

Once you start to see this, your whole world will change. You won't take your thoughts so seriously. You will be less reactive and less fearful.

Sometimes, you will even laugh out loud at those thoughts because wow, they do go on a bit don't they?

Please don't get me wrong. I am not vilifying the mind. It's such a useful tool. It's needed to navigate our way through the everyday world of functions and roles.

But through meditation you can come to know that the mind is not the center of everything. You will come to rest in that which sees the comings and goings, the untouched expansiveness of awareness itself.

When you meditate, you simply sit or lie down comfortably. Relax. Take a big breath in, through the lungs and into the belly . . . and release.

Feel the sensations at the soles of your feet. There may or may not be tingling. Be aware of any sensations but without labeling them or judging them . . . . Simply feel.

Continue moving your awareness up your body in this way: lower leg, upper legs, hips and pelvis, lower torso, upper torso, upper arms, lower arms, shoulders, neck, and head.

Take your time. Let the thoughts come and go, as they will, without hanging onto them and without pushing them away.

Beginners to meditation sometimes find this uncomfortable. They are bombarded with the voices, thought after thought after thought.

Some of these thoughts have more momentum than others and try to suck you in. These charged thoughts can be very uncomfortable or emotional.

Just breathe. Shift your attention back to your body; to how it meets the floor or the chair you're sitting on—feeling the breath come into your lungs and your belly.

Just be present in the moment and you'll find the thoughts will have less of a charge and will begin to lose momentum. Don't judge; just be accepting of it all.

After a while you will start to notice something. You will start to rest more in the space that has seemingly been created but which, in reality, has always been present.

You will find that you are identifying less with the thoughts and resting more in yourself: the vastness of that in which your thoughts and experiences come and go.

If you're still struggling with meditation, as I did when I first started, I suggest you try the Osho active meditations I mentioned earlier. They work better and faster than any other meditation method I've tried.

You could also try putting on your favourite music, setting it to play for about 15 minutes and dancing with wild abandon until it stops . . . then simply sitting or lying down and sinking into the silence.

Mindfulness is similar to meditation, only with your eyes open and in the playground of life. It is like taking meditation into the world around you.

Mindfulness is synonymous with awareness. It's being present in the moment, it is resting in awareness while eating, talking, thinking, and experiencing is going on around you and within you.

Mindfulness is being aware, moment-to-moment, of your thoughts, feelings, body sensations and environment . . . without any judgment of good, bad, right, wrong.

Personally, I found mindfulness much more difficult than meditation because there are sooo many more distractions out there in the world versus when I'm lying in meditation on my bed in the quiet of my bedroom with my eyes closed.

I found that, at first, I couldn't stay mindful for more than a few minutes at a time. This is where the grounding technique I spoke about in the beginning of this book came to the rescue.

I tweaked it a little for when I was out in the world. I found that bringing up the energy all the way through to the crown of my head was not practical.

So I simply felt the energy in the soles of my feet and let it rest there as I went about my daily business. I didn't put my whole focus into it, instead just knowing that it was there in the background, keeps me grounded and aware and spacious.

Sometimes I would bring the energy up to my womb. For the guys reading this, bring your energy up into your balls. This is particularly powerful when public speaking, or when confronted with someone who is angry, or any situation that brings fear.

In these situations, when I forget to womb-ground, my voice can become shaky and higher pitched. My breath can be shallow and I speak from a more contracted voice box.

When I speak from my womb, there's a strength that pours forth. I can hear it in my voice. It's lower, stronger and more confident. My breath is deeper and I feel that others hear me far more readily than when I forget to "womb centre".

In any event, I just got into the habit of grounding or centering more and more, in all different situations. It instantly puts me in the present, allowing for things to come and go within a vast awareness.

It's such a simple technique and yet so sublimely profound. I'd practice grounding while I was in the queue at the bank or while I was shopping in the supermarket.

I'd practice it when I stopped for coffee. I'd practice it on the toilet, in the shower, or as I picked up the phone. I'd discover that food tasted better, I'd be more sensitive and empathetic to people, I'd appreciate colours and smells more deeply, and I'd be less caught up in thoughts and more attuned to what was happening in the here and now.

What grounding does for me is help me fall into mindfulness with ease. And the more I did this, the more easily it came, the more natural it became. There was less of the 'practicing' of mindfulness because mindfulness, or awareness, became naturally more present . . . and in fact, IS ever present . . . we just need to get out of our own way!

Chapter Ten:
Tuning in to the Body

By now you are perhaps seeing a common thread throughout this book. Grounding, somatic therapy, meditation, mindfulness . . . they all include the body in some way.

It's ironic really. On the one hand, I know I am more than this body, much more than this mind. I am that which is aware of the body and mind. And yet, the body has been and continues to be, a vehicle to awareness, an anchor for awareness.

So it makes sense to tune in to the body. It makes sense to become aware of its sensations, to look after it with healthy food and beneficial treatments and exercises like massages, bodywork, Yoga, Chi Kung and Tai Chi.

Ahhhhhh . . . massages. If I could afford it, I would have a massage several times a month, like I did in Bali. Although I must say, it takes a bit of trial and error and asking around before you usually find a good massage therapist.

There are so many different techniques and so many practitioners; some excellent and others, not so much. It's always better to ask for recommendations, find out who people are going to, what technique is used, how their bodies respond to the massage, if they go back, etc.

A good massage will clear blocked energy, allow Prana energy to flow, increase circulation and oxygen to the cells and reduce all kinds of pain from muscle pain to headaches to frozen shoulders, sciatica, back pain, sports injuries and sprains.

Massages also eliminate toxins and radically reduce stress, which is the number one cause of disease in the body. Not only that, they make us feel good!

When I started caring for myself enough to include regular massages, my general well-being improved immensely. Even when I was going through financially challenging times, I found ways I could get a massage. I was able to source free massages.

You can exchange service for service. Some massage therapists are open to this. What are you good at? What can you exchange for receiving a massage? There's always a way.

Tai Chi, Chi Kung and Yoga are all ancient mind-body practices that produce more energy than they consume. Doing any one of these practices will help us feel calm, clearheaded and invigorated because they work on all levels . . . body, mind and spirit.

By deepening the mind-body connection with mindful breathing, postures, stretches and meditation, these ancient practices encourage our innate healing capacities to bloom.

My favourite practice of all, though, is walking in nature. One of the best things we can do for ourselves is walking outside, away from noise and concrete and cars and people and wireless waves.

Walking on a quiet beach or along a river or in the forest is tremendously beneficial to our well-being. Nature has a way of clearing our heads, connecting us to the earth, and grounding us.

We instinctively know how good nature is because of the way we are attracted to animals, flowers, and water. We spend time and money to have more of that in our lives by the gardens we create, the pets we love, the ponds we build, the trees we plant, and the vegetables we grow.

Just ask any keen gardener and they'll tell you why they do it . . . because it's soul food!

So taking a walk in a natural setting is something we're all intrinsically drawn to and we always feel good after spending time in it.

There's a wonderful book called Claim Your Wildness by a friend of mine, Dr. Les Higgins, a health educator and researcher with extensive experience in bushwalking and other outdoor activities. It's well worth reading.

The book blends science, personal observation and experience to explain:

- Why we need to have regular contact with nature
- What nature can contribute to our health, well-being and quality of life
- How everyone can enjoy the gifts that nature offers.

The book leaves the reader no doubt that "few elixirs have the power and punch to heal, restore, and rejuvenate the way that nature can."

Chapter Eleven:
Relationships

Now, for the chapter I believe many of you have been waiting for. Hands up all those who are perfectly fine until they get into a relationship?

With such a high divorce rate, it would seem that traditional relationships are being phased out. People are no longer willing to work things out amongst themselves.

Whether you are for or against staying in a marriage or long-term relationship, the fact of the matter is that traditional relationships are failing. The reason? Well, because traditional relationships are built around personal gratification.

What inevitably happens is that, in an effort to work things out, compromises are made, and partners try to change themselves to appease the other. Due to this, they start to feel boxed in and no longer free to be themselves. They lose the sense of who they are in an effort to maintain the relationship.

Traditional relationships are all about staying in the comfort zone, about pleasing the other and not rocking the boat. Much is repressed.

Partners feel stifled as they tend not to express their feelings, their hopes, and their dreams. They tend to take the "let sleeping dogs lie approach" to their past too, so past traumas and fears don't get to be aired out in the open to be seen for fear of judgment.

It's no wonder that traditional relationships are breaking down. It's rather wonderful in fact. The world is birthing a new form of relationship . . . the conscious relationship.

In a conscious relationship, the focus is on growth.

It's about speaking out and sharing what's going on with us. It's staying in the room when things get uncomfortable.

It's about not taking things personally when the other is upset. If they're upset, it generally means they're caught up on something, not you.

It's allowing them their freedom of expression, allowing them to see for themselves where they're caught up.

It's about anchoring yourself in awareness, grounding and breathing whenever there's a disturbance or incident and taking the lens from a sharp to a soft focus.

Be gentle on yourself and your partner. To succeed you must be kind to each other and yourself. You must be willing to be vulnerable.

I know it's not always comfortable but when the focus is on growth, rather than comfort or maintenance of the status quo, you're like a team. Both of you supporting each other in your growth.

One thing's for sure. We can positively, absolutely count on our partner to continually remind us what is unresolved in ourselves.

So rather than buying into the traditional relationship where the emphasis is on comfort and "working on the relationship," we would do well to see our relationship "working for us" . . . as a way to grow.

For this shadow self, the unresolved parts of us, long to be brought into awareness.

Consequently, we are triggered more and more and this can be excruciatingly painful to bear unless . . . unless . . . we are graced with a shift in perspective.

Unless both parties use the relationship to transform themselves and use the depth of intimacy as a means to come closer to themselves, only then can you grow with each other. For in truth there is nothing outside of ourselves (but that's another book right there).

Imagine a relationship where we remove the burden we place on our partners to take care of those parts of ourselves we have disowned or hidden.

Imagine an intimacy that has no expectations of constant joy, constant connection, or even a port for the weary to be safe from the world.

Growth may not always be safe or comfortable. The mind wants safety and comfort but growth can be messy and often (momentarily) painful. Growth yearns for the unseen and unresolved to be seen and held and integrated.

So . . . go for growth! Do not be afraid. And if you are, feel the fear and do it anyway! Be vulnerable, be human, and be sincere in your quest for awakening.

Be two people moving forward together, in their honesty and integrity and vulnerability, as a team with a purpose. Growth! The rewards are too vast to even imagine.

One more thing I want to touch on here is the question of soul mates. Is there such a thing as a soul mate?

Certainly for me, those unresolved pains led me to an endless search for a soul mate to make things right. It is only now that I know that it wasn't a soul mate I needed, that all I really needed was to be seen and held.

A soul mate is not someone who you meet and stay with for the rest of your life. It could be, but not necessarily so.

A soul mate is someone who you instantly recognise at your core as you.

It can be the briefest glance of a stranger that stills the mind and reminds you of your own essence. It's the outpouring of love in an instant as you remember who you are through the reflection in another's eyes.

There is no mind in that. There is only the timelessness of being. There is no two in that, there is only one.

In truth, we are all soul mates. And even that isn't the truth, for "mate" suggests that there are two, when deeper than that, we are one. There is only one, appearing as many.

Chapter Twelve:
Love

Love . . . . Our *raison d'être*!

When we talk of love, the majority of people think of romantic love. While this is the stuff most movies are made of, the reality is that love has less to do with another person and much more to do with us.

"So where is the part about unconditional love in the relationship chapter?" a friend of mine asked when she read the draft of this book. It's a fair question, so why did I feel a bit uncomfortable with it?

You're supposed to love unconditionally, aren't you? Isn't that what you're going for? Well, I don't think it's as simple as that.

You see, love is unconditional but relationships are not. Whatever your expectations are of your partner (fidelity, honesty, transparency), there's usually trouble when these expectations aren't met.

Does this mean when he lies to me, I suddenly don't love him? Not at all. It just means that a trust has been broken and the relationship may or may not survive.

Sure, mistakes are made and we're here to grow. We talk, we hash it out, we sit in the fire of the lie, we feel the sensations in the body, we allow, we grow . . . all good. But if there are more lies, I'm probably gone.

So is this a condition of my love for him? No, it's a condition of my relationship with him. I know that I'd rather be alone than in a relationship with someone who is not transparent and honest.

The problem about this question of unconditional love, as noble as it is, is that we personalize it and by its very nature, it's not a personal thing at all.

Existence itself is unconditional love. While we can be vessels through which it operates, when we demand unconditional love of ourselves, and others, we are simply pushing ourselves further away from it.

Serving others is an outward extension of love. After about four months of living in beautiful Ubud, I got a phone call from my Dad in Perth, Australia.

He sounded exhausted, like he could barely summon up his voice to speak. Not surprising since Mum has Alzheimer's. Even with all the home care help I put into place before I left for Bali, it clearly wasn't enough.

It was time to go home and look after my parents.

Had you told me just a few short years ago that I would volunteer to move into my parents place and look after them in their old age I would have said "not bloody likely."

Dad always said that when the time came, they would happily move into an aged care home, so it never occurred to me that the reality would be different. But you see, Dad wasn't ready a year ago when we first talked about it because he was still reasonably fit and energetic.

However, in just one short year, as he crept towards 85, his health had declined rapidly. It's tough mentally and physically, looking after someone with Alzheimer's, and at his age, it had started to wear on him. So I flew home.

The reason I'm telling you this is that I can't believe that I would enjoy being there for them as much as I do.

That it is an honour to be cooking and shopping for them. It's a privilege to be making them cups of tea all day long. To be sitting with them at "drinky" time watching the clouds, listening to old time foxtrot music, watering their garden and talking and laughing about old stories (the only time frame Mum really remembers).

I never thought that being of service to them and taking care of them would have a sweetness to it that I had never experienced before. It's total role reversal—they cared so well for me all those years ago, now it was my turn to care for them.

Let me be clear. I could not take on this commitment simply out of obligation—that's not my style. I have always believed that obligation breeds resentment.

Yet, here I am, doing it out of genuine love for them and a desire that they live as long as they can in the house they built together.

Being of service can be its own reward. I never really got that till now.

Sure, there are times when I'm tired or fed up, but those are just clues to balance things out . . . balancing the "being kind to others" with "being kind to ourselves."

The instant I find myself becoming irritated, that's my cue to take time for me. I make a date with a friend, go to lunch or watch a movie. Refreshed, I once again fall in love with my parents, happily doing for them what they can no longer do for themselves.

Love is who we are. It's our true nature. Awakening to our true nature is perhaps the most radical evolutionary step a human being can make.

There is no need to be loved, for we are love itself.

Love is not an emotion, it can't be conjured up with the mind, and it doesn't have an "opposite".

Love is that place we rest in when watching a sunset or leaning, eyes closed, against an ancient tree.

It's the quiet depth of another's eyes. It's puppy dogs and kittens and babies of all kinds.

It's a place of deep silence, of quiet bliss. It's infinite and vast and always present. It's there in every breath we take.

Love is very simply the spacious, open attention of our awareness.

It's not something to be found, but something to be uncovered. Rumi says it best with "your task is not to seek for love, but merely to seek and find all the barriers within yourself that you have built against it".

Endnote

Now, there's something that needs to be clarified before I'm finished with this book. While I have had great revelations and deep healings and I continue to do those things that make me lighter and freer and more heart-centered, I am by no means saying that peace and happiness is a constant.

I have been through enough to know that the more I grow, the more open I am to meeting the next shadowy part of myself. So although I say I am free, that is more an acknowledgment of a healing or of an awakening . . . with the caveat that I am still human, I still have "stuff" that, at any moment can suddenly arise . . . even more so now because I am no longer resisting these things.

So do not suppose that my journey is now over or that I'm impervious to pain. In fact, I am more sensitive and vulnerable than I've ever been.

It's just that now I am no longer triggered in ways that I used to be. Now, when something does come up, a flash of anger, or fear or hurt, I know that the body has its own intelligence.

So there is more of a willingness to open up to uncomfortable feelings when they arise. There is a willingness to be aware of the sensations in the body, and to allow the feelings and sensations space rather than shuffle them in some corner to be dealt with some other time.

Emotions move through with greater ease and so fast sometimes that it makes me smile.

I am also much more free in the way I live my life. I live more spontaneously than I used to and am much more intuitive too.

You know, I haven't worked a nine to five job in over 20 years. I have the freedom to live anywhere in the world, not because I'm rich, far from it, but simply because I listened to my intuition.

I wanted to work when I felt like it, not be tied to a particular time frame. I wanted to be able to travel more.

So I learned new skills and created a small social media business for myself that I love, doing work for people who I love, that doesn't tie me down to one particular place.

Becoming conscious affects your whole life and allows you freedoms you didn't even know you had.

I hope that in sharing some of my stories, from little tips to profound insights, that you will be inspired to live your life in truth and freedom.

Go, explore the depth of yourself. No need to overwhelm yourself with trying everything at once. Just choose one thing at a time; whatever piqued your interest most when you were reading.

It took me over 30 years to explore these practices. Just start somewhere.

Find people who you can be authentic with.

Meditate. Dance. Sing.

Be grateful. Be mindful. Be present.

Hug a tree. Plant a tree. Grow some herbs and veggies.

Climb a mountain. Swim in a clear blue ocean. Get a massage.

Go do a personal development workshop.

Find a spiritual teacher who holds Satsangs and sit with them a while.

Find a somatic therapist and release known and unknown early traumas so that you can truly be free.

Find the lover and be the lover who is not willing to take the burden of the other's unresolved issues but rather, lovingly returns this task to the one who so desperately yearns to be free.

Find and be the partner who allows the space for the other to be seen. Be there to hold them when that happens.

Co-create a truly conscious relationship . . . or just be single and in love with yourself.

Hang out with those who are aligned with growth and have the same deep resonance for freedom and the same joy in the exploration of moment-to-moment awareness.

A Special Gift

FREE 20 minute Guided Meditation

REST IN THIS THAT YOU ARE:
A Guided Meditation in Resting as
Awareness

From the audio: "You are much more than the body, much more than the mind. You are awareness itself. All there really is, is a sense of presence. When a thought arises, it is only a movement. No need to follow it. You are simply the space in which all movements happen. Like the sky. Clouds come and go like thoughts, but the sky is always present.

You are just here like the ever present sky..."

Download from here:
http://livelifehappy.today/meditations/

About the Author

Since this book is about the processes, experiences and insights I've had, you already know me quite intimately so I have nothing to add except to say that it is my heartfelt wish that you discover who you really are and live the life you were meant to live.

If you would like to get in touch with me, I actually do answer emails from readers. Please write the title of this book in the subject heading. My email is melaniedilday@gmail.com

If you enjoyed this book, I would be grateful if you could tell your friends and leave a review on Amazon. Even a brief review will be greatly appreciated.